Believe and Achieve

This edition published by Parragon in 2011

Parragon
Queen Street House
4 Queen Street
Bath BA1 1HE, UK

Internal design by Pink Creative Ltd

ISBN: 978-1-4454-3766-8

Printed in China

Believe and Achieve

A Collection of Inspirational Thoughts and Images

Bath • New York • Singapore • Hong Kong • Cologne • Delhi
Melbourne • Amsterdam • Johannesburg • Auckland • Shenzhen

If you can imagine it,
you can achieve it.

If you can dream it,
you can become it.

William Arthur Ward, Writer

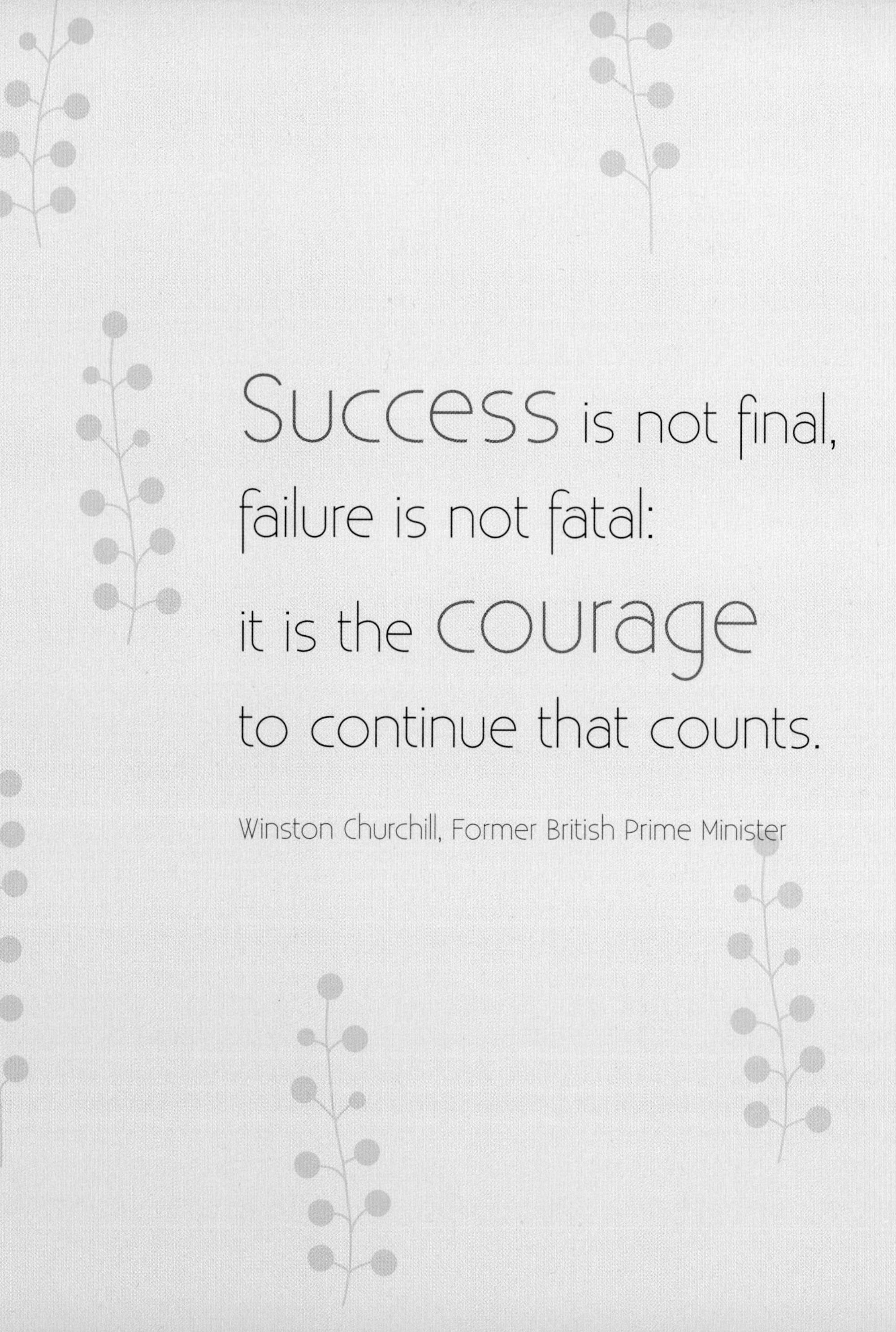

Success is not final,
failure is not fatal:
it is the courage
to continue that counts.

Winston Churchill, Former British Prime Minister

Those who contemplate
the beauty of the earth
find reserves of strength
that will endure
as long as life lasts.

Rachel Carson, Ecologist

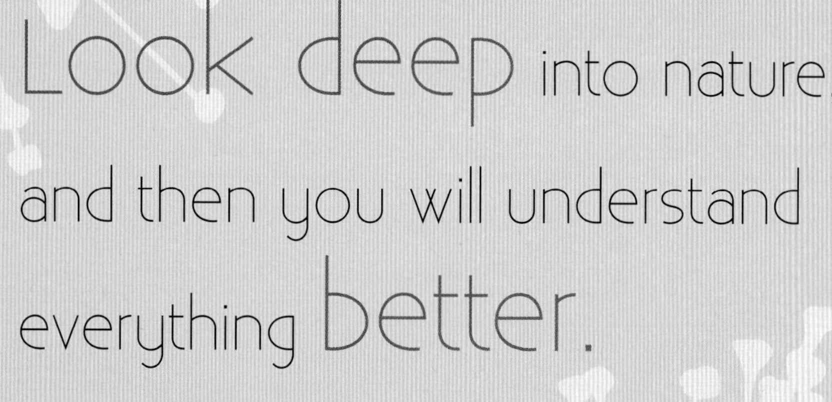

Albert Einstein, German physicist

The person who makes a success of living is the one who sees his goal steadily and aims for it unswervingly—that is dedication.

Cecil B DeMille, Film producer

The journey
of a thousand miles
must begin with
a single step.

Lao Tzu, Ancient Chinese philosopher

In the midst of winter,
I found there was, within me,
an invincible summer.

Albert Camus, French author

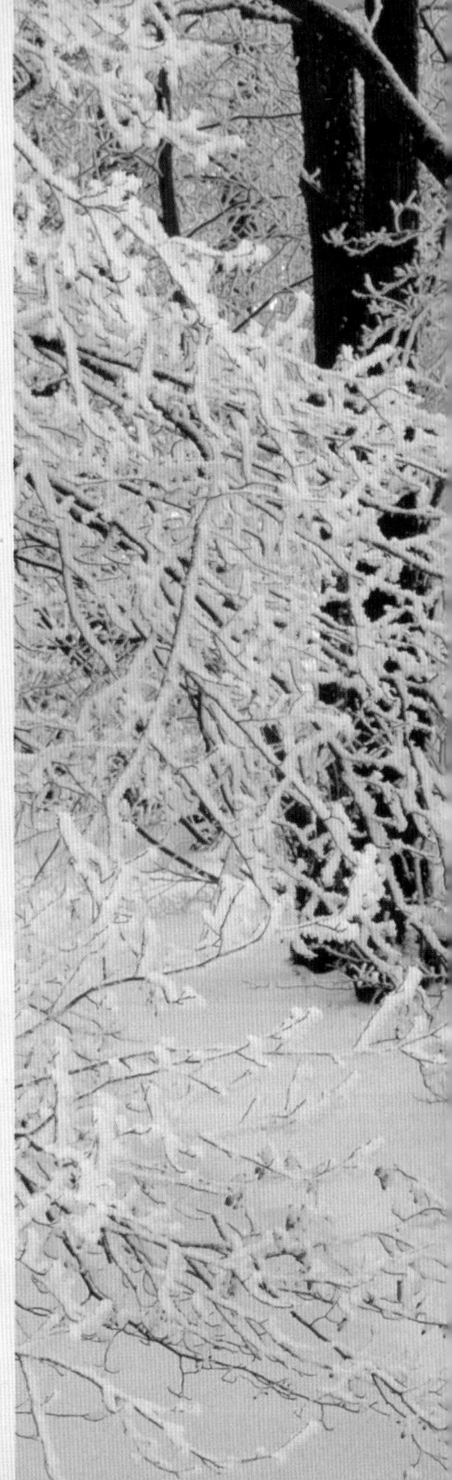

Whatever you can do or dream you can, begin it.

Boldness has genius, power and magic in it!

Johann Wolfgang von Goethe, German writer

The clearest way into the universe is through a forest wilderness.

John Muir, Botanist

Man cannot discover new oceans
unless he has the courage
to lose sight of the shore.

Andre Gide, French author

Make each day

your masterpiece.

John Wooden, Sportsman

Don't judge each day by the harvest you reap

but by the seeds that you plant.

Robert Louis Stevenson, British novelist

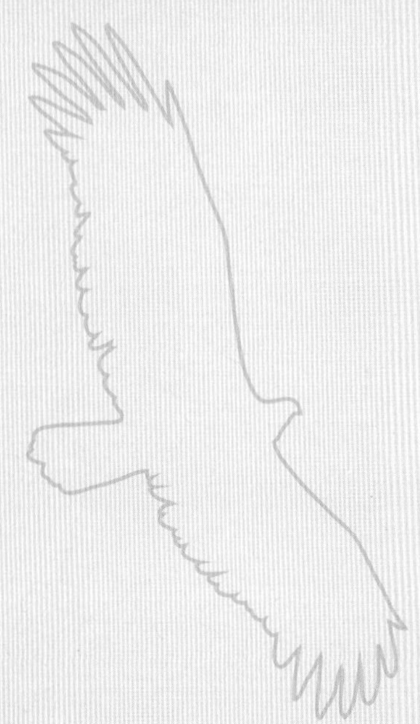

To climb steep hills requires
a slow pace at first.

William Shakespeare, British poet and playwright

Hope, like the gleaming taper's light,
adorns and cheers our way;
And still, as darker grows the night
emits a brighter ray.

Oliver Goldsmith, British author

Giving up doesn't always mean you are weak.
Sometimes it means that you are strong enough to let go.

Unknown

Destiny is not
a matter of chance,
it is a matter of choice.

William Jennings Bryan, Politician

Do not go where
the path may lead,
go instead where
there is no path
and leave a trail.

Ralph Waldo Emmerson, Essayist

There is a way that nature speaks, that land speaks. Most of the time we are simply not patient enough, quiet enough, to pay attention to the story.

Linda Hogan, Poet and novelist

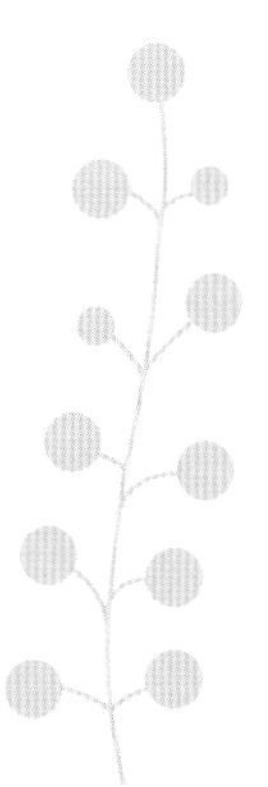

Hope is like a road in the country;
there was never a road, but when
many people walk on it,
the road comes into existence.

Lyn Yutang, Chinese writer

If you have built castles in the air,
your work need not be lost;
that is where they should be.
Now put foundations under them.

Henry David Thoreau, Author

You cannot plough a field
by turning it over in your mind.

Unknown

Don't count the days,
make the days count.

Muhammad Ali, Boxer

Happiness often sneaks in through a door

you didn't know you left open.

John Barrymore, Actor

The steeper the mountain

the harder the climb

the better the view

from the finishing line.

Unknown

Forget the times of your distress,

but never forget what

they taught you.

Herbert Gasser, Physiologist

To fall into a habit
is to begin to cease to be.

Miguel de Unamuno, Spanish essayist

Kind words can be short and easy to speak

›ut their echoes are truly endless.

Mother Teresa, Roman Catholic Nun and humanitarian

In the hopes of reaching
the moon men fail to see the flowers
that blossom at their feet.

Albert Schweitzer, German theologian

Have a heart that never hardens,
a temper that never tires,
a touch that never hurts.

Charles Dickens, British novelist

...without darkness, nothing comes to birth,
As without light, nothing flowers.

May Sarton, Poet

Life is not about waiting
for the storm to pass.
It's about learning
to dance in the rain.

Unknown

The journey is
the reward.

Chinese proverb

Live as if you were to die tomorrow
Learn as if you were to live forever.

Mahatma Gandhi, Indian political and spiritual leader

Try and fail,

but don't fail to try.

Stephen Kraggwa, African entrepreneur

Your worth consists in

what you are

and not in

what you have.

Thomas Edison, Inventor

You gain strength, courage, and confidence by every experience in which you really stop to look fear in the face. You must do the thing which you think you cannot do.

Eleanor Roosevelt,
First Lady from 1933–45

You may only be

someone in the world,

but to someone else,

you may be the world.

Enrich Fried, German poet

Believe and act as if it was impossible to fail.

Charles Kettering, Inventor

To accomplish great things
we must not only act,
but also dream;
not only plan,
but also believe.

Anatole France, French poet

Happiness is where we find it, but rarely where we seek it.

J Petit Senn, French-Swiss poet

Yesterday is but today's memory, and tomorrow is today's dream.

Khalil Gibran, Lebanese-American artist

Only those who will risk going too far can possibly find out how far one can go.

T S Eliot, Poet and playwright

Happiness held is the seed;

Happiness shared is the flower.

Unknown

You can't do anything about the length of your life, but you can do something about its width and depth.

Evan Esar, Humorist

The difference between the impossible and the possible lies in determination.

Tommy Lasorda, Sportsman

And in the end it's not the years
in your life that count.

It's the life in your years

Abraham Lincoln, President from 1861—1865

Picture credits

pp. 4-5 © Yasushi Akimoto/Getty; pp. 6-7 © Anzeletti/iStock; pp. 8-9 © Rich Reid/Getty; pp. 10-11 © Don Smith/Getty; pp. 12-13 © Katsuhiro Yamanashi/Getty; pp.14-15 © Dennis Hallinan/Getty; pp.16-17 © Jan Tove/Getty; pp.18-19 © Romaoslo/iStock; pp. 20-21 © AVTG/iStock; pp. 22-23 © Walter Bibikow/Getty; pp. 24-25 © Ingmar Wesemann/Getty; pp. 26-27 © Dave Reede/Getty; pp. 28-29 © Gordon Wiltsie/Getty; pp. 30-31 © Eerik/iStock; pp. 32-33 © manfredxy/iStock; pp. 34-35 © Gary Yeowell/Getty; pp. 36-37 © Light, perspective and life...all that matters/Getty; pp. 38-39 © Tino Soriano/Getty; pp. 40-41 © Chris Harris/Getty; pp. 42-43 © Comstock Images/Getty; pp. 44-45 © JayKay57/iStock; pp. 46-47 © Michael Coyn/Getty; pp. 48-49 © isitsharp/iStock; pp. 50-51 © A330Pilot/iStock; pp. 52-53 © ooyoo/iStock; pp. 54-55 © Roine Magnusson/Getty; pp. 56-57 © Tom Fowlks/Getty; pp. 58-59 © Don Smith/Getty; pp. 60-61 © Christopher Seufert Photography /Getty; pp. 62-63 © George Kavanagh/Getty; pp. 64-65 © DFeinman/iStock; pp. 66-67 © OG/iStock; pp. 68-69 © Angelo Cavalli/Getty; pp. 70-71 © Rich Reid/Getty; pp. 72-73 © Mlenny/iStock; pp. 74-75 © DeanBirinyi/iStock; pp. 76-77 © Nigel Blythe/Getty; pp. 78-79 © meldayus/iStock; pp. 80-81 © Gareth McCormack/Getty; pp. 82-83 © Raimund Linke/Getty; pp. 84-85 © Richard Nowitz/Getty; pp. 86-87 © H, & D. Zielske/Getty; pp. 88-89 © Shigeki Fujiwara / Sebun Photo /Getty; pp. 90-91 © Shaun Egan; pp. 92-93 © TVAllen_CDI/iStock; pp. 94-95 © Adam Jones/Getty.